SPEAK TO YOUR PET

My Guide To Cat Training

Ashley Lee

Explore other books at:
WWW.ENGAGEBOOKS.COM

VANCOUVER, B.C.

e➜ WWW.ENGAGEBOOKS.COM

My Guide to Cat Training: Level 2
Speak to Your Pet
Lee, Ashley 1995 –
Text © 2022 Engage Books
Design © 2022 Engage Books

Edited by: A.R. Roumanis
Design by: A.R. Roumanis

Text set in Arial Regular.
Chapter headings set in Arial Black.

FIRST EDITION / FIRST PRINTING

LIBRARY AND ARCHIVES CANADA CATALOGUING IN PUBLICATION

Title: My guide to cat training / Ashley Lee.
Other titles: Cat training
Names: Lee, Ashley, 1995- author.

Identifiers: Canadiana (print) 20210371749 | Canadiana (ebook) 20210371757
ISBN 978-1-77476-655-2 (hardcover)
ISBN 978-1-77476-656-9 (softcover)
ISBN 978-1-77476-658-3 (pdf)
ISBN 978-1-77476-657-6 (epub)

Subjects:
LCSH: Readers (Elementary).
LCSH: Readers—Cats—Training.
LCSH: Readers (Publications).

Classification: LCC PE1119.2 .L44 2022 | DDC J428.6/2—DC23

This project has been made possible in part by the Government of Canada.

Canada

Contents

Why Should I Train My Cat?

Training your cat can help keep them safe. Walking your cat on a leash instead of letting them run freely outside can help stop accidents. Using a cat carrier can help you safely take them to the vet.

Training your cat is also a good bonding experience. You and your cat will become closer and enjoy living together even more.

SAFETY TIP:

Always have an adult supervise your training sessions to make sure you and your cat are staying safe.

What Is My Cat Trying to Tell Me?

Happy cats keep their ears pointing forward and their mouths closed.

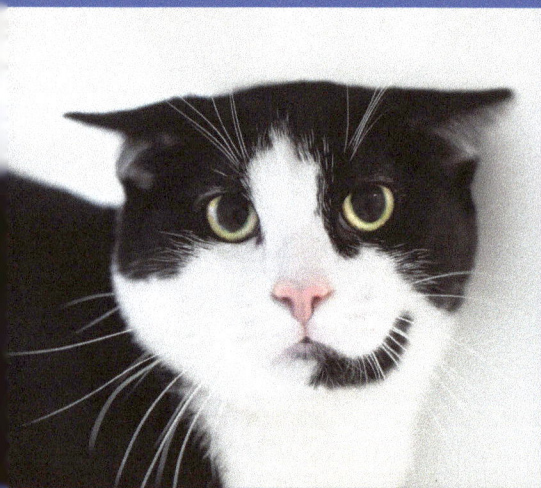

An angry cat will flatten its ears against its head and their whiskers will point backwards.

A worried cat will turn their ears sideways and tuck their head into their body.

6

Happy cats hold their tails upright. If they show you their belly, that means they trust you.

An angry cat will arch its back to make itself look bigger. Their whole body will be tense.

A worried cat will keep its tail close to its body and crouch down low.

What Is the Best Way to Train My Cat?

Practice makes purr-fect, so set aside ten minutes every day to work with your cat. Don't worry if your sessions are shorter in the beginning. Make sure you're in a quiet area with few distractions.

Just like people, all cats have different needs. This means it may take longer for some cats to learn. If you or your cat are getting irritated, stop your training session and try again another day.

SAFETY TIP:
Never yell at your cat or hit them. This can cause them to bite or scratch you.

What Tools Do I Need to Train My Cat?

Lots of healthy treats: Make sure your treats are small so your cat doesn't get too full.

Clicker: A clicker is a small device with a button that makes a clicking sound when you press it.

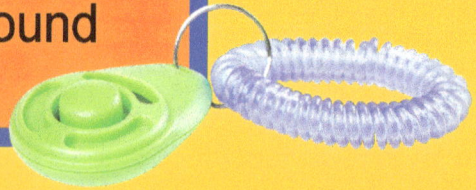

Toys: Use toys instead of treats if treats don't make your cat excited.

Cat carrier: Make sure your carrier is the right size for your cat. A carrier that is too small will be uncomfortable for your cat. A carrier that is too big may cause your cat to go to the bathroom in it.

Scratching post: A scratching post helps prevent your cat from scratching the furniture.

SAFETY TIP:

Pay attention to your cat's body language. Stop your training session if your cat is showing signs of fear or anger.

Beginner Lesson 1: Charging Your Clicker

Charging your clicker means getting your cat used to it so they know the click sound means they get a treat. Here is how to charge your clicker.

1 Give your cat a treat and click the clicker at the same time. Repeat four or five times.

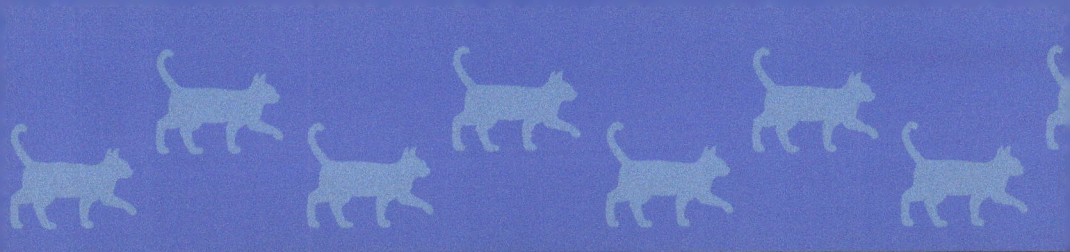

2 Next, click the clicker first, then toss the treat in front of your cat so they have to move to get it. Repeat four or five times.

3 Repeat steps 1 and 2 for several days in a row. Now click the clicker and see if your cat looks at you for a treat. If they do, you're ready to move on. If not, repeat the steps for a few more days.

Beginner Lesson 2: Come

1 Sit close to your cat, hold out your hand, and say "come." If your cat comes to you, click and give them a treat. If they don't come, move closer and try again. Repeat four or five times.

2 Move a few steps back and repeat step 1. Repeat four or five times.

3 Repeat every day, moving farther away from your cat as they improve.

Beginner Lesson 3:
Using a Scratching Post

1 Place some toys around the scratching post. Encourage your cat to play with the toys.

2 If your cat scratches or climbs the scratching post during your play session, click your clicker and give them a treat.

3 If your cat doesn't scratch or climb the post, try dangling a toy near the top of the post so your cat has to climb to get to it.

4 Repeat these steps every day until your cat starts to use the scratching post on their own.

Beginner Lesson 4: Using a Carrier

1 Place a towel in the carrier. Leave the open carrier on the floor for several days to let your cat get used to it.

2 Place a treat on the towel at the back of the carrier. Click your clicker when your cat steps on the towel and eats the treat. Repeat three or four times.

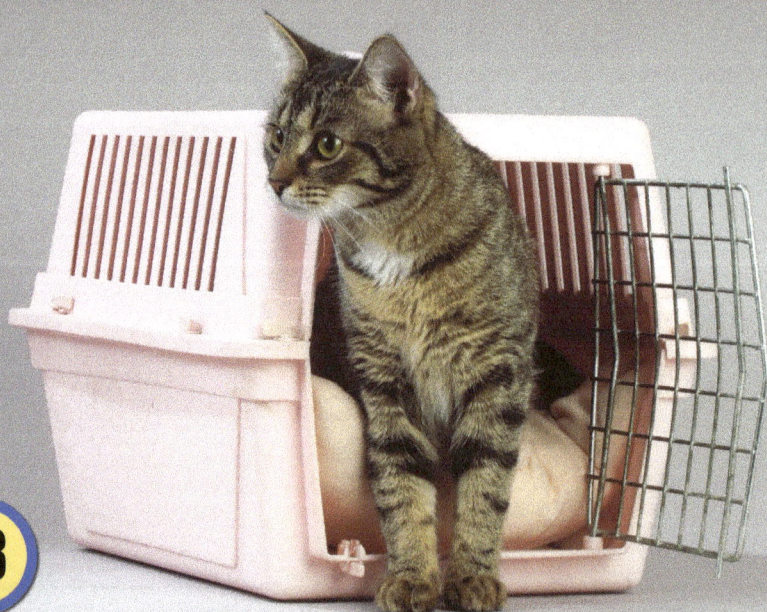

③ Repeat step 2, closing the door a bit more each time over several days. When your cat is comfortable with the door being fully closed, leave them in the carrier for about one minute before rewarding them with a treat.

④ Slowly increase the amount of time you leave your cat in the carrier.

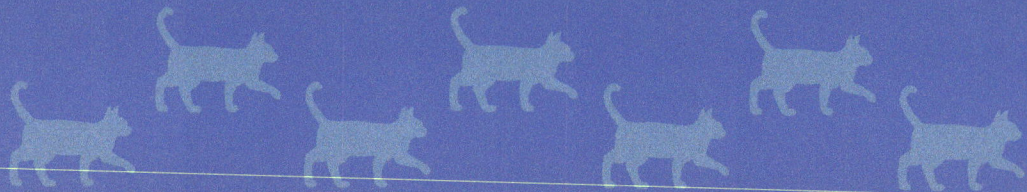

Advanced Lesson 1: Sit

1 Sit in front of your cat. Hold a treat in front of your cat's nose and slowly move it up.

2 Your cat will follow the treat with its eyes. As they tilt their head up, their back end will lower until they are in a sitting position.

3 Say "sit" while clicking the clicker and giving your cat a treat. Repeat steps 1 through 3 four or five times a day for several days.

4 Click the clicker and say "sit" without holding the treat in front of your cat. If they sit, give them a treat. If they don't, repeat steps 1 through 3 for a few more days.

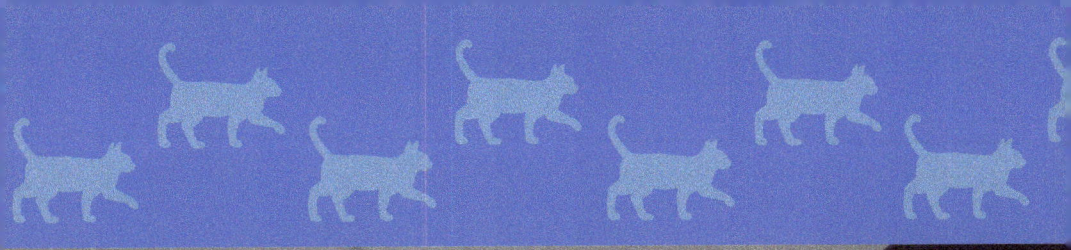

21

Advanced Lesson 2: High-five

1 Hold a treat in front of your cat.

2 When your cat touches your hand with their paw to try to get the treat, click the clicker and give them the treat. Repeat 4 or 5 times for several days.

3 Offer your cat your hand without holding a treat. If your cat high-fives you, click and give them a treat. If not, repeat steps 1 and 2 for a few more days.

4 Offer your cat your hand while saying "high-five." If your cat high-fives you, click and give them a treat. If not, repeat step 3 for a few more days.

Advanced Lesson 3: Wearing a Harness

1 Leave the harness out for a few days so your cat can inspect it and get used to it.

2 Lay the harness across your cat's back. This will help them get used to the feeling. Take it off and put it back on four or five times a day for a few days.

3 Give your cat a treat while you put the harness on properly. Leave it on for 2 to 3 minutes and give them another treat when you take it off.

4 Slowly increase the amount of time your cat wears the harness each day as they get used to the feeling.

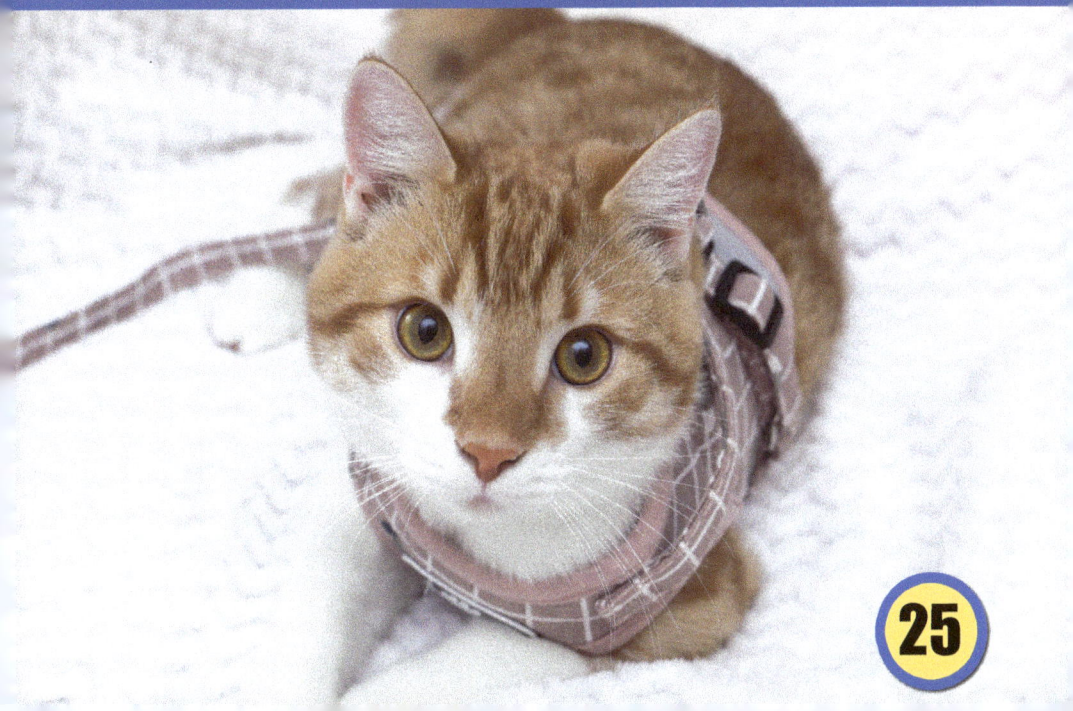

Advanced Lesson 4: Walking on a Leash

1 Put your cat's harness on and attach a leash. Let your cat walk freely around the house for a few minutes. Repeat for several days.

2 Follow your cat while holding the leash. If they start to pull away too much, stop walking and ask them to sit. Give them a treat when they listen.

3 Now have your cat follow you on the leash. Make sure to give them lots of treats when they don't pull away. Repeat steps 2 and 3 for one week.

4 When your cat is comfortable walking on a leash inside, you can try taking them outside for a few minutes. Pick a quiet area with few distractions. Increase the time as your cat becomes more comfortable.

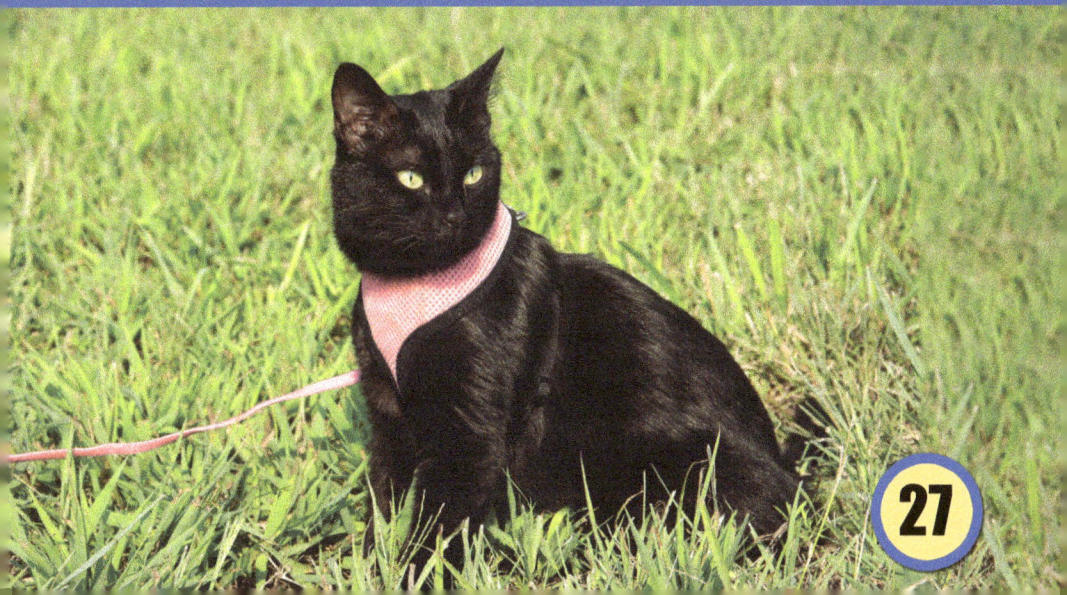

Super Training

With enough time and patience, cats can be taught to do some amazing tricks. Here are some of the craziest cat tricks you and your cat can work towards!

Some cats have been taught to use a toilet instead of a litter box. No more messy clean-ups for their owners!

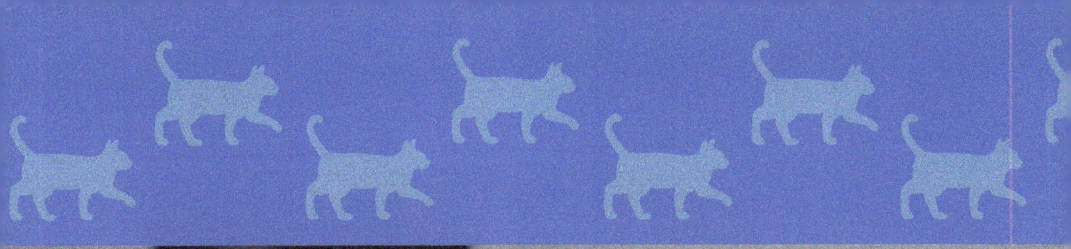

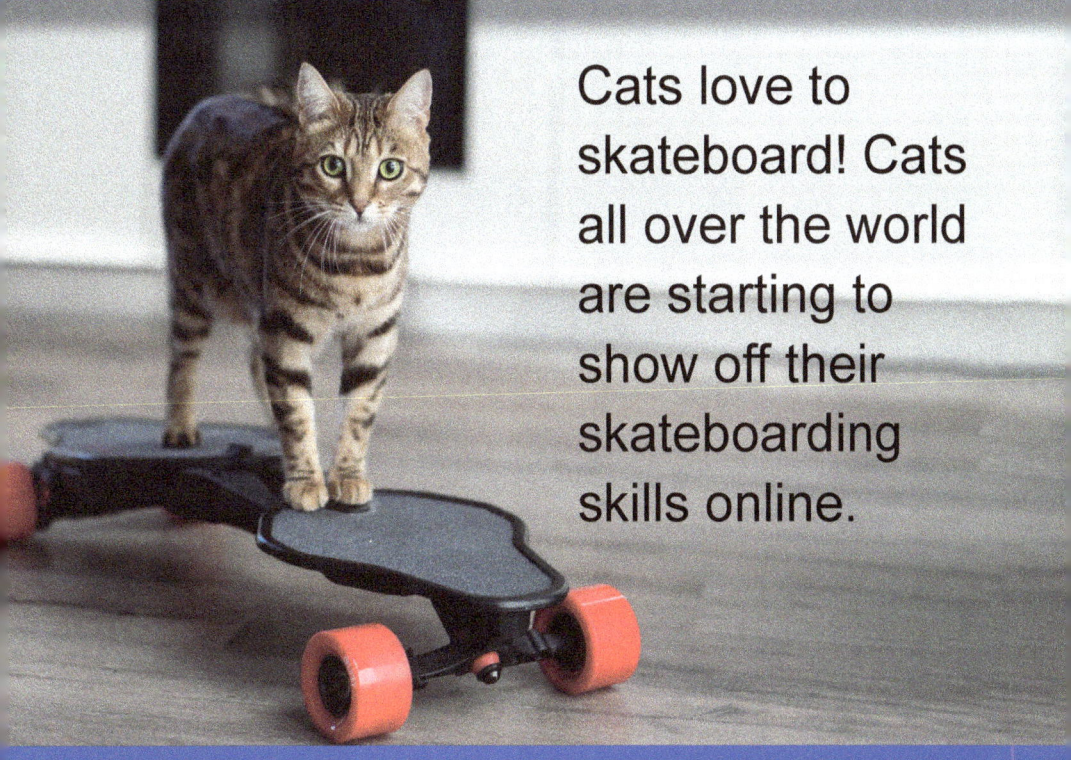

Cats love to skateboard! Cats all over the world are starting to show off their skateboarding skills online.

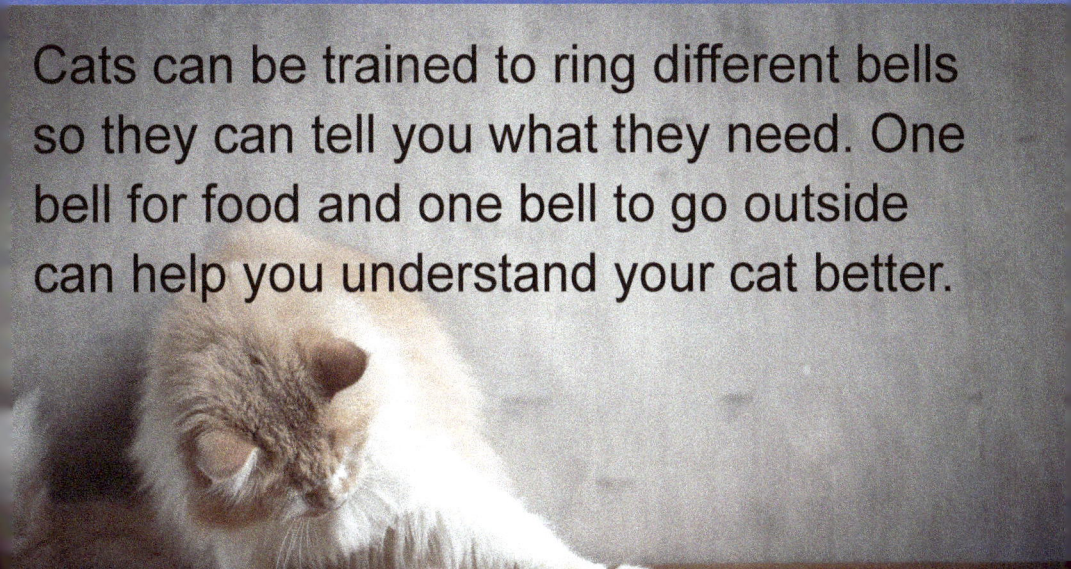

Cats can be trained to ring different bells so they can tell you what they need. One bell for food and one bell to go outside can help you understand your cat better.

Quiz

Test your knowledge of cat training by answering the following questions. The questions are based on what you have read in this book. The answers are listed on the bottom of the next page.

1 Why should an adult always supervise your training sessions?

2 What does it mean if a cat flattens its ears against its head?

3 What does it mean if a cat holds its tail upright?

4 Why should you use small treats when training your cat?

5 What is a clicker?

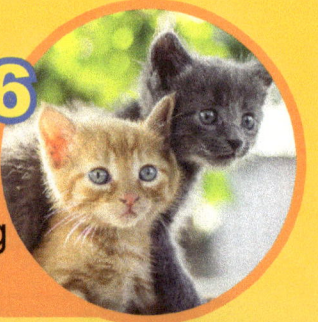

6 What should you do if you or your cat are getting irritated during a training session?

Explore Other Level 2 Readers.

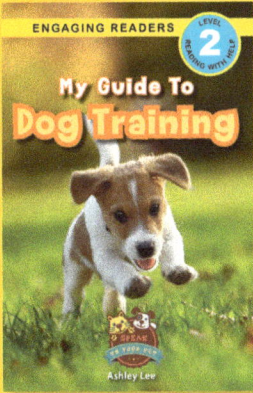

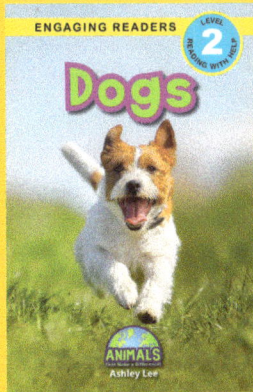

Visit www.engagebooks.com/readers

Answers:
1. To make sure you and your cat are staying safe 2. It is angry
3. It is happy 4. So they dont get too full 5. A small device with
a button that clicks 6. Stop and try again another day

www.ingramcontent.com/pod-product-compliance
Lightning Source LLC
Chambersburg PA
CBHW051238020426
42331CB00016B/3434